Jazz Up Your Journal Writing

Grades 5–6

by
Dr. Phyllis J. Perry

Carson-Dellosa Publishing Company, Inc.
Greensboro, North Carolina

Credits

Editor:
Amy Gamble

**Layout Design
and Art Coordination:**
Jon Nawrocik

Inside Illustrations:
Stefano Giorgi

Cover Design:
Peggy Jackson

ISBN 0-88724-195-6

Table of Contents

What is the purpose of journals in the classroom?

Journals can be one of several tools used to evaluate student learning. Journal entries can provide regular information, not only about the quality of a student's writing, but also about a student's thoughts and understanding in various subject areas. Journal writing that follows prompts like those included in this book can be exciting and satisfying to students and can serve as a valuable curricular tool.

Students need to understand that classroom journals are not private diaries. They should be aware from the beginning exactly how the journals will be used and who will be reading them. You may choose to read and comment on your students' journal entries. Or, journal entries might be shared with the class or a small group or lead to an oral discussion on a topic of interest.

How should journals be incorporated into class time?

Journal writing is most effective if it appears as a regular activity throughout the school week. You may select a time each day or two or three times a week for students to write in their journals. The length of writing sessions may vary, although 15 or 20 minutes seems to work well for elementary grade students. The period right after lunch is especially popular because it serves as a time for students to be quiet and settle down.

Sometimes journal writing might be unstructured. During these times, students may be invited to write whatever they wish, including their thoughts and feelings. But, often it is more useful if the journal writing is structured with a specific assignment. The assignment might be selected from this book, or it may be one that you originate that is centered around a particular subject, season, holiday, or current event.

How should journal entries be graded?

The decision to read and grade student journals is left to your discretion. Often, students will write more freely and enjoy journal writing more with the knowledge that their work will not be read or judged. However, if the journal is to be used for assessment purposes, at least reading and possibly grading would be necessary. Just be sure to let students know what the parameters are up front.

You should also consider the time involved in reading each student's journal. When only one or a few children are involved in a home-schooling situation, journal reading can easily be accomplished. In a school setting, it is advisable to read through about one-fifth of the classroom journals at a time. This way, the task does not become overwhelming.

Introduction

In order to give students practice in writing to communicate and to express their ideas and emotions, you may want to allow students to write freely without worrying about spelling. Correct spelling and vocabulary building can be addressed by having students keep personal dictionaries to which they can refer during journal writing time. You may also display a word wall or word lists related to topics being studied.

How should students' journals be made and organized?

To complete the activities in this book, each student needs a personal journal. The pages in this book are reproducible with space for students to write (including the backs of copied pages). It is recommended that each student use a three-ring binder as a journal. Then, pages can be copied and added as they are assigned, or all of the pages can be placed in the journals at the beginning of the year and completed as assigned. Photos or student artwork can be used to decorate the covers.

For ease of reading and grading journals, each student can add two blank pages to the beginning of his or her journal to use as a table of contents. Students can number their journal pages in the upper right hand corners; give titles to their stories, articles, and poems (or use the titles from the prepared prompts); and list these titles and page numbers in their tables of contents.

Several copies of the blank, programmable journal page (page 48) can be added to the end of each student's journal for unstructured writing. Or, you can use this page to write your own prompts and make copies for each student. You may also give individual students the opportunity to write journal prompts for the class.

About this book:

Jazz Up Your Journal Writing is full of suggestions to help teachers and home-schooling parents incorporate student journal writing into all four areas of the core curriculum—language arts, math, science, and social studies. The activities also address writing in both poetry and prose forms. Some pages offer literature suggestions for students to read that serve to introduce, extend, and enhance the lessons. Have these and/or other relevant books checked out from the library and available to students in the classroom as they complete the activities.

Most of the journal activities can be completed without additional materials or instruction. Any additional preparation or information needed is noted in the *Tips and Extensions* section (pages 6–7). Extensions for more in-depth writing or project ideas for activities are also included in this section.

Through a Visitor's Eyes (page 8): Have each student choose one activity from his or her list and write a postcard about completing this activity with a guest. Let students cut out postcards from poster board, write about the activities on the backs, and draw pictures of them on the fronts.

Advertising Slogans (page 9): Allow students to perform their advertisements for the class. You may wish to videotape students so they can watch themselves and critique their ads.

Book Jacket Copy (page 10): Provide books of historical fiction, like those suggested on the journal page. After completing the journal activity, have students write complete stories based on the book jacket copy.

Diamante Poems (page 11): Compile students' poems into a class book. Make a copy of the book for each student to take home and enjoy.

Proverbs (page 12): After completing the journal activity, have students write their own proverbs. Or, challenge students to research various proverbs to find their origins.

Letter to the "Editor" (page 13): Let each student refine his or her letters and publish two to five each week. Distribute or post the editorial page in the school and encourage other students to write responses.

Lost and Found (page 14): Allow students to make their flyers by hand or on a computer. You may wish to complete this activity early in the year and display the flyers on a get-to-know-you bulletin board.

Tricky Triplets (page 15): After students have practiced writing triplets, ask them to write triplets to show their knowledge and understanding of newly-learned material or to tell about books they read.

Favorite Sneakers (page 16): Gather books about sneakers, like those listed on the journal page. Have each student choose one situation from his or her list and write a full story about it.

Jargon Dictionary (page 17): Bind students' dictionaries together in alphabetical order by topic and use as a classroom reference.

Red Herrings (page 18): Let students exchange papers and solve each others' problems.

Dream Vacation (page 19): Challenge students to lower the costs of their vacations. Have them replan their trips and economize wherever possible.

Comparing Days (page 20): Have each student write sentences to show their comparisons. For example, "I spend $1/4$ of a day more at school than I would like to."

Map Miles (page 21): After completing the journal activity, ask each student to choose one city and plan a car trip to that city, including driving directions.

Using Math (page 22): Use students' ideas from their journals to create a bulletin board display for the school called "Math Every Day."

Explaining Data (page 23): Ask each student to write an explanation for why he or she chose a certain type of graph to represent the data.

Valuable Sentences (page 24): Develop a class list of letter values and see who can write the most valuable words and sentences.

Serving Thirty (page 25): Provide a variety of recipe books for students to review. See the journal page for suggestions. After completing the journal activity, have each student reduce the servings of his or her recipe to feed just two or three people.

Yummy Problem (page 26): Let each student respond to a classmate's report as if he or she were the president of Yummy Candy Company.

Picture It! (page 27): After completing the journal activity, encourage students to write original problems and draw pictures to prove the correct answers.

Clouds (page 28): Gather books about clouds for the classroom, like those listed on the journal page. Ask students to record the appearance of the clouds for a two-week period. Have them record the temperature and weather conditions each day, as well. Then, let students check their journal predictions with the recorded data to see if their predictions match their observations.

Ways to Conserve (page 29): Have students use the lists from their journals to make brochures promoting the conservation of electricity. Let students distribute their brochures around the school.

Environmental Cartoon (page 30): Display students' cartoons on a bulletin board in the school.

Constellations (page 31): After completing the journal activity, ask students to write myths about how their constellations came to be.

Earthquakes (page 32): Provide books about earthquakes, like those listed on the journal page. Let students work in pairs to present dramatic interpretations of their journal entries.

Alike and Different (page 33): Have students imagine what their grandchildren might look like and be like. As they write the descriptions, encourage them to consider what traits and abilities their grandchildren might inherit.

Sound Waves (page 34): Ask each student to choose a sound from the journal activity and explain why he or she chose to draw the sound wave that way.

Observation of a Tree (page 35): Challenge students to write poems about their trees.

Endangered Species (page 36): Provide students with access to the Internet and books about endangered animals. Allow time for research.

Writing Hypotheses (page 37): Let students conduct their experiments and compare their results to their hypotheses. Encourage students to graph their results and write about why the results matched or did not match their hypotheses.

Nose for News (page 38): Compile students' articles and create a school newspaper. Encourage other students in the school to submit articles, too.

Geographic Words (page 39): Have each student write a story about being a visitor from outer space and exploring one of the geographic features from the list.

The Good Old Days (page 40): Encourage students to write about how they think life will change in the next 100 years.

The 13 Colonies (page 41): Share books about life in the American colonies, like those listed on the journal page.

Reuse It! (page 42): Have students write stories about what life might be like if nothing was reused and everything was thrown away.

Historic Figures (page 43): Let students practice their public speaking skills by reading their entries to the class.

Wanted (page 44): Provide students with access to the Internet and/or library. To explore various careers, have students write want ads for other occupations.

World Contributions (page 45): Allow students access to the Internet and/or library. Provide time for research.

Stamp Hero (page 46): Challenge students to write poems in honor of their stamp heroes.

Wagons Ho! (page 47): Share books about Americans traveling west in the 1800s. See the list on the journal page for suggestions. Let students write and illustrate their own picture books about traveling in covered wagons.

Through a Visitor's Eyes

Most of us take for granted the history and interesting sites in and near our hometowns. Imagine that someone from out of town is visiting for a week and you must plan a week of sightseeing and other things to do. Below, write a schedule for the week that includes all of the things that you think are important to do and see in your town.

© Carson-Dellosa

Advertising Slogans

What are some of your favorite commercials? What makes a commercial effective? Does it have a memorable slogan or jingle? Is it funny or exciting? Make up a product such as a soft drink, snack food, toy, or game. Then, write a 30-second television commercial for the product. Include a catchy song or slogan and an interesting story or visuals that would appeal to a young audience.

© Carson-Dellosa

Book Jacket Copy

Historical fiction is fiction that is based on real events in history. Look at the inside flaps of book jackets from several historical fiction books, like those listed below. Book jacket flaps often give a summary of what a book is about without giving away too many details or the conclusion. Plan to write a story of historical fiction by writing book jacket copy. Your copy should include the main character(s), setting, and basic plot.

Thunder at Gettysburg
by Patricia Lee Gauch
(Boyds Mill Press, 2003)

Across Five Aprils
by Irene Hunt (Berkley Publishing Group, 1987)

Behind Rebel Lines: The Incredible Story of Emma Edmonds, Civil War Spy
by Seymour Reit (Gulliver Books, 2001)

© Carson-Dellosa

Diamante Poems

Many types of poetry have a certain structure within which to be creative. A diamante poem follows a diamond pattern. A specific number and certain type of word must be used on each line. The first and last lines of a diamante poem are words that are either closely related or are opposites, and the poem flows from describing the first subject to describing the last subject. Follow the pattern shown below to create your own diamante poem.

© Carson-Dellosa

One-word subject
Two adjectives describing the first subject
Three *-ing* words describing the first subject
Four nouns—first two relate to first line; second two relate to last line
Three *-ing* words describing the last subject
Two adjectives describing the last subject
One-word subject

Proverbs

Proverbs are common sayings of wisdom that can be used to describe a variety of situations. Some examples of proverbs include: *Time is money. You can't teach an old dog new tricks. You can't eat your cake and have it, too.* Choose a favorite proverb and explain what it means. Then, give your opinion on whether you agree with the proverb and tell why or why not.

Letter to the "Editor"

A letter to the editor is a letter written to and published by a newspaper that expresses a reader's opinion. Read several letters to the editor in your local newspaper. Then, write a letter to the "editor" (your teacher or school principal) about something school-related that you have a strong opinion about—good or bad. Keep in mind that the most effective letters of complaint offer suggestions to improve the problem.

© Carson-Dellosa

Lost and Found

Pretend that you have lost three items that are very important to you. In order to find the lost articles, you decide to hand out flyers to see if anyone has found them. Below, write the text for your flyer. Describe each item in detail, and include when you last had each item and why it is so important to you. You may wish to include a reward for each item.

Tricky Triplets

Triangular triplets look deceptively simple, but take some thought to write. In most poems there are definite first lines, second lines, and so on. In a triangular triplet, the poem is written along the edges of a triangle and is designed to be read starting from any point on the triangle. All three lines of the poem should rhyme. Look at the example below, then try writing one or two of your own.

Stark against the blue sky stand the trees.

The autumn season is sure to please.

Orange, red, and golden hang the leaves.

Favorite Sneakers

Imagine that your favorite pair of sneakers could talk. What wild stories might they tell of the adventures they had while traveling around on your feet? Where did they go? What did they do? Did they step in something gross? Were their laces always untied? Write a list of things your sneakers might have said at various points in their lifetime. Some of your entries might be more in-depth than others.

Nasty, Stinky Sneakers by Eve Bunting (HarperTrophy, 1995)

A Pair of Red Sneakers by Lisa Lawston (Orchard Books, 1998)

Yesterday I Lost a Sneaker by David M. McPhail (Silver Press, 1995)

© Carson-Dellosa

Jargon Dictionary

Are you an expert on a certain topic, like baseball, computers, or art? If so, then you probably know certain words that are specific to that topic. These words are called jargon. Think about something you know a lot about or learn about a new subject. Write down a list of all of the jargon used when talking about that subject. Then, write a definition for each jargon vocabulary word.

© Carson-Dellosa

Red Herrings

Solving a math story problem is a lot like being a detective. Just like a detective in a mystery story, you must find clues to solve the problem. Often a mystery story includes clues, called red herrings, that are meant to send the detective in the wrong direction. You sometimes see red herrings in math story problems, too. Write a mystery math story problem that includes all of the necessary clues to solve the problem, but also includes several red herrings.

© Carson-Dellosa

Dream Vacation

If you could go anywhere on vacation for a week, where would you go? Write a short paragraph describing your dream vacation. Now, come back to reality and find out how much your vacation would cost. Use the Internet to find information on plane fares, cruise fares, lodging, car rental, etc. Remember to include money for food and entertainment. Total the costs to determine the budget for your dream vacation.

© Carson-Dellosa

Comparing Days

Divide the page down the middle. On the left, write the number of hours you would spend in an ideal day sleeping, eating, working at school, doing homework, watching television, doing chores, etc. On the right, write the number of hours you actually spend on the same activities. Make sure each day adds up to 24 hours, then translate each time into a fraction of hours in a 24-hour day. Compare your ideal times to your actual times.

Map Miles

Where in the world does an inch equal a mile? On a map! Look at a road map. Find your city and then choose several cities you would like to visit. On the map, determine how far away each city is in inches from your home city. Then, use the map scale to convert each measurement to miles (or kilometers). Which city do you think you could drive to in a day? How long do you think it would take to drive to the city that is farthest away?

SCALE

SCALE IN MILES

SCALE IN KILOMETERS

© Carson-Dellosa

Using Math

How many ways is math used in real life? Write a list of all of the instances you can think of when numbers, computation, geometry, measuring, etc., are used in everyday life. Then, write a paragraph about a time when you used math outside the classroom. What was the situation? What math skills did you use? Describe the event and how you solved or handled the situation using math.

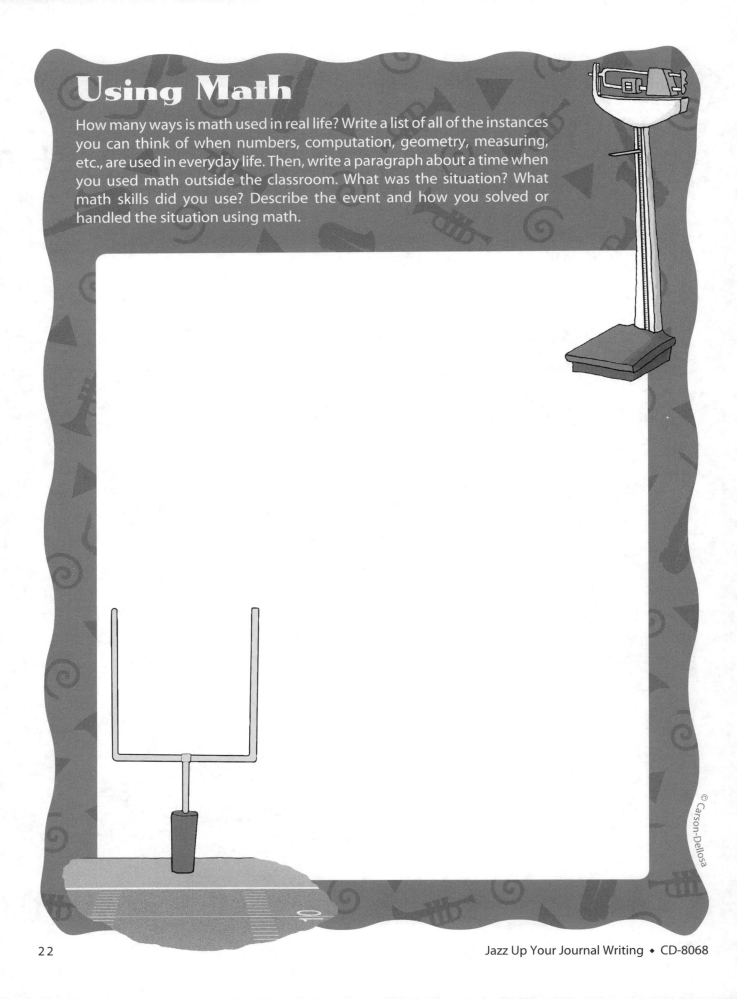

© Carson-Dellosa

SPORTS

NUMBER 1

Explaining Data

Look at the sports page in a local newspaper. Examine a set of statistics, such as the wins and losses of the baseball teams in a certain division, and create a graph to represent the data. Choose the type of graph that would best show the data. Then, write a short sports article to explain the data about the current standings of those teams. Use the back of the page if you need more room.

Valuable Sentences

Assign each letter of the alphabet a money value. Make each vowel worth 25¢. Then, assign values to the remaining letters, making the less frequently used letters (like q, z, and x) worth more. Next, find the value of your name. Write a sentence and find its value. Try to write the most valuable sentence possible—but make sure it makes sense.

© Carson-Dellosa

Serving Thirty

Look through some recipe books, like those listed below, and choose a recipe that serves fewer than eight. Write the ingredients from the recipe below, including the measurements. Then, imagine you will serve this recipe for a party with 30 guests. How much of each ingredient will you need? Convert the recipe ingredients to accommodate 30 servings and write the new ingredients list below or on the back of the page.

50 Recipes for Kids to Cook by Judy Williams (Gallopade Publishing Group, 1990)

Betty Crocker's Kids Cook! by Betty Crocker Editors (Betty Crocker, 1999)

Better Homes and Gardens Step-by-Step Kids' Cookbook by Better Homes and Gardens Staff (Meredith Books, 1985)

© Carson-Dellosa

Yummy Problem

Yummy Candy Company has hired you to do some market research for them on two new candies. Read the problem below. Then, write a report to the president of Yummy Candy Company that gives your recommendation for which of the new candies they should sell and why. Consider factors that might have influenced customers, variation in the market experiments, and the possibility that additional research may be required.

Yummy Candy Company wants to know which new candy to offer in concession stands at movie theaters. As an experiment, a chain of five movie theaters showing the same films, offered the new candies for sale. Only one kind of new candy was sold at any theater. Cherry Dreams were sold for three weeks in two theaters. Chocolate Delights were sold for two weeks in three theaters. During that period of time, 672 boxes of Cherry Dreams were sold and 840 boxes of Chocolate Delights were sold.

© Carson-Dellosa

Picture It!

Communication is important in math. You must know how to communicate through numbers, words, and pictures. Read the following problem: Bill ate $\frac{2}{3}$ of a pizza. Mary ate $\frac{2}{3}$ of another pizza. Bill insisted that he ate a lot more than Mary. Mary said they ate the same amount. Can they both be right? Draw a picture representation to prove one or both of the students' statements.

© Carson-Dellosa

Clouds

There are many different types of clouds. Observe the sky for several days or look at clouds in books, like those listed below. On the journal page, draw pictures of at least four different types of clouds. Then, below each picture, write your prediction for the type of weather there would be if that type of cloud were in the sky. Take it further by including the scientific name for each cloud type.

Cloud Dance
by Thomas Locker
(Silver Whistle, 2000)

The Everything Kids Nature Book by
Kathiann M. Kowalski (Adams Media Corp., 2002)

DK Guide to Weather by Michael Allaby
(Dorling Kindersley Publications, 2000)

© Carson-Dellosa

Ways to Conserve

By burning fossil fuels to make electricity, we not only use nonrenewable natural resources, but we also pollute the environment. Using alternative sources of power, such as water, sun, and wind, is one way to help the situation. Another way is to conserve the amount of electricity we use. Write a list of at least 20 things that you can do to use less electricity every day.

© Carson-Dellosa

Environmental Cartoon

Political cartoons are found in most newspapers. The cartoonist gets across his or her political view or position with a drawing and very few words. To get a feel for political cartoons, you may wish to look at a few in old newspapers or on the Internet. Think of an environmental issue, such as the greenhouse effect, the extinction of certain animals, air pollution, etc., and draw a political-style cartoon about it.

SAVE the TREES PLEASE!!

Constellations

Make a list of as many constellation names as you can think of. Then, choose one constellation to write about. Use what you already know, or do research using the Internet or the books listed below. Draw a picture of your constellation, label the names of its major stars, and write at least three interesting facts about the constellation.

See the Stars
by Ken Croswell
(Boyds Mill Press, 2000)

National Audubon Society First Field Guide: Night Sky
by Gary Mechler (Scholastic, 1999)

Constellations by E. M. Hans
(Raintree/Steck Vaughn, 2000)

© Carson-Dellosa

Earthquakes

Think about the effects of an earthquake. If you need more information, read some books about earthquakes, like those below. Based on what you know about earthquakes, and maybe some information about famous earthquakes, write an imaginary diary page written the day after an earthquake. Describe the event, the damage, and what will happen next.

Earthquakes by Ellen J. Prager (National Geographic Society, 2002)

Earthquake! by Cynthia Pratt Nicolson (Kids Can Press, 2002)

Earthquakes by Neil Morris (Bt Bound, 1999)

© Carson-Dellosa

Alike and Different

Many of our characteristics are inherited from our parents, while some others are the result of our experiences and our interactions with the environment. Think about the types of characteristics that are inherited versus learned. Write a list of your traits that you believe were inherited from your parents and a list of traits that you think you learned through experience and interaction with your environment.

© Carson-Dellosa

Sound Waves

Sound travels in waves. Sound waves vary depending on their loudness, pitch, pleasing or displeasing tone, etc. A basic sound wave is shown below. The dips can be larger, smaller, closer together, farther apart, irregular, and so on. Choose ten sounds, some pleasing, some displeasing, some loud, some soft. For each sound, draw a picture of what you think the sound wave would look like.

Observation of a Tree

Effective scientists must be good observers and communicators. Practice these skills by recording your observations of a tree at school or at home. Choose a tree to study and write down everything you observe about the tree—size, shape, leaf size and shape, seed, flower, animal life, etc. Include a sketch of your tree. Then on the Internet, research to identify your tree's type.

© Carson-Dellosa

Web sites about trees:

www.enature.com/guides/select_trees.asp

www.oplin.lib.oh.us/products/tree

www.arborday.org/trees/treeID.html

Endangered Species

There are many endangered species in the world, and some might even be found in the area where you live. Make a list of some animals that are endangered. Use the Internet or books if you need help generating your list. Divide the animals on your list into land animals, birds, and sea creatures. Then, choose one animal and write a plan for how people can help save that species.

© Carson-Dellosa

Writing Hypotheses

Choose a general topic that you are interested in and that you could collect data about, such as favorite sports, ice cream flavors, television shows, types of music, etc. Write a hypothesis, or educated guess, about the preferences of students in your school. Then, write a plan for how you would conduct an experiment to test your hypothesis. How many students do you think you would need to poll to support your hypothesis?

© Carson-Dellosa

Nose for News

Look at some examples of articles from a newspaper. Write the title of the article and then identify *who* the story is about, *what* happened, *when* it happened, *where* it happened, and *why* it happened. Then, choose an interesting event at your school, such as an author visit, an upcoming field trip, or an athletic event, and write a newspaper article about it. Be sure to report on who, what, when, where, and why.

WHO? WHAT? WHEN? WHERE? WHY?

THE DAILY TIMES

BELIEVE IT!

Geographic Words

There are many different kinds of geographical features on Earth. Each of these features has a specific name. Look at the list of geographical features below. Then, imagine you are a visitor from outer space and are exploring Earth for the first time. You do not know the names for these geographical features, so you must give them new names based on what they look like to you.

© Carson-Dellosa

bay
canyon
continent
cove
crater
delta

desert
fjord
geyser
glacier
island
isthmus
lake
mountain
ocean

peninsula
plateau
river
valley
volcano

The Good Old Days

How has life changed from the early 1900s to the early 2000s? What kinds of new technology, advances in science, changes in attitudes, etc., have there been? Do you think the changes have been for the better? Have any been for the worse? Write a list of changes in the past 100 years and indicate whether you think the change was for the better or worse. Choose one worse change and explain your thoughts about it.

© Carson-Dellosa

The 13 Colonies

Imagine that you live in England in the mid-1700s. You want to move your family to America. Since there are 13 colonies and each is very different, you must decide which one to move to. In making your decision, consider climate and natural resources, products, jobs, and imports of the colony. Also consider type of food available, type of government, rules, and religious practices. Use the books suggested below to help you decide.

The American Colonies by Jeanne DuPrau (Kidhaven, 2001)

Read more about the colonies!

The South Carolina Colony by Tamara L. Britton (also by Britton, *The Maryland Colony*) (Checkerboard Library, 2002)

The Colonies by Rebecca Stefoff (Marshall Cavendish Corp., 2000)

© Carson-Dellosa

Reuse It!

Recycling trash and reducing the amount of trash we produce are both ways to help the environment. Another way is to take an object that was used for one purpose and would be thrown away, and reuse it for another purpose. Choose one of the objects listed on the trash can below and write a list of at least 20 other uses or things you can make from that object.

newspaper
soup can
six-pack rings
cardboard box
cereal box
grocery bag
milk jug

© Carson-Dellosa

Historic Figures

Choose a person from history that you know a lot about, or use the Internet or library to research a historical figure. Then, pretend you have been asked to introduce this person at a banquet in his or her honor. A good introduction would describe this person's achievements, obstacles that needed to be overcome, humorous and tragic moments, etc. Write your speech below.

© Carson-Dellosa

Wanted

What qualities does it take to be the leader of a country? Brainstorm a list of these qualities and number them in order of importance to you. What are the legal requirements for this position? Use the Internet or library for more information. Use this information and the list of qualities you generated to write a want ad for a president or prime minister.

WANTED: LEADER OF THE FREE WORLD

Looking for experienced leader to run government operations for large, well-known nation. Frequent international travel

© Carson-Dellosa

World Contributions

Over time, people from many different countries have enriched life by contributing inventions, great works of art and music, special foods, games, stories, ideas for governing, etc. Choose a country and write a list of the contributions of the people from that country that you already know about. Then, use the Internet or research in the library to find out more.

© Carson-Dellosa

Stamp Hero

Throughout history, people have been recognized for their achievements in statesmanship, the arts, sports, science, etc., by having their images printed on stamps. Write a list of at least six people you think deserve to have their faces on stamps. Then, choose one and write a letter suggesting that a stamp be made to commemorate this person. Explain what accomplishments make him or her worthy of this honor.

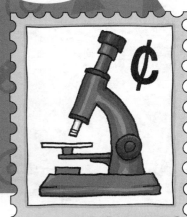

M. Jones
100 Green St.
Evergreen, CO 13356

DENVER, CO 133
PM
31 MAY
2003

Mr. L. Jones
155 Chapmans Ave.
Warwick, RI 02889

© Carson-Dellosa

Wagons Ho!

In the 1800s, many Americans moved west by covered wagon. These settlers faced many hardships during their travels and as they tried to establish new settlements. Imagine that you are in a wagon train heading west to start a new life. Write a diary entry to record some of your imaginary experiences on the wagon trail. Use the books listed below to help you imagine what it might have been like.

Covered Wagon Women by Kenneth L. Holmes (University of Nebraska Press, 1995)

If You Traveled West in a Covered Wagon by Ellen Levine (Scholastic, 1992)

Daily Life in a Covered Wagon by Paul Erickson (Scott Foresman, 1997)

© Carson-Dellosa